The Recovery Manual

The Recovery Manual

A Guide to Post-Scandal Redemption

Pastor Andre D. Jones

Jones House Publishing
Chesapeake

Book Design by Andrea Smith | Smith Brown Press

Cover Design by Adrian Taylor | Ayden's Lab Designs, LLC

ISBN: 978-0-578-24759-5

Jones House Publishing 2021

Email: pastoradjones@gmail.com

The Recovery Manual: A Guide To Post-Scandal Redemption is a book of breakthrough! This book not only tells you how to recover, but it leads you through sound doctrine on how to stay free. This is a Kingdom book for Kingdom citizens living in true redemption!!!

Bishop Brandon A. Jacobs Sr.
New Zion Temple Church
Hammond, IN

Pastor Andre Jones is what I believe to be one of the most innovative Kingdom minds of our generation. Our present church culture is often sitting on the porch of social media waiting for the next church scandal to take place. Jones, in this vibrant read, pinpoints the nuisances of these situations that often go unaddressed. This book doesn't just examine the fruit but analyzes the root. The author in his new book will prove why WE can't afford to keep him anonymous.

Bishop S. Y. Younger
Ramp Church International
Lynchburg, VA

Pastor Andre Jones is a phenomenal gift to the Body of Christ and the world at large. This book is just enough to engage us in championing the desire of sanctification and godly habits again or for the first time. It helps the reader to see their flesh as is. Identifying its flaws but encouraging us to look to the Holy Spirit as a perpetual agent of renewal and change.

Dr. Aaron Hannah
South Church
Baltimore, MD

Dedication

I am humbled, careful and cautious with great intentionality to dedicate this body of work firstly to my wife Chelsea. You've stood faithfully with me in every venture and adventure since our blessed nuptials. I've learned that hardly anything is possible without your love. Thank you, Sweetheart, for such an abundance of your heart, your prayers and support.

Acknowledgments

To the many supporters who have encouraged me to write down through the years and close friends who've sternly encouraged me to the degree of possible argument, I am indebted to you for this inaugural work (blog-book) and the many others to come. Last, but not least, to Ms. Andrea Smith, Chief Editor of Smith Brown Press who has been such a superb encouragement and faithful guide throughout this process.

Foreword by Bishop Jason Nelson

The current culture of the world is accustomed to the idea of "canceling" any individual or concept that is deemed inappropriate based on current circumstances. This culture of eliminating a person who has erred offers little space for recovery to occur. This is not the biblical model to which we must adhere. The bible is replete with examples of people who have made egregious mistakes and still found a doorway to forgiveness and recovery. Because we follow the Bible and its precepts, we must learn the functions of recovery and being restored.

Andre Jones has encapsulated this concept. To know that my last mistake doesn't cancel God's purpose for my life is both comforting and refreshing. To know that a public scandal cannot erase the purpose that was spoken over my life before my entrance into the world (Jeremiah 1:5), gives me the courage to face my decision and still find a way to emerge as a victorious believer.

As you read this book, take into account that God cannot be overwhelmed with what overwhelms us. He cannot be taken by surprise concerning our proclivities and penchants for engaging in undesirable behavior. He knows our faults and decisions before we make them and has set up a remedy for our ills. Know that we serve a GOD who can be touched with the feelings of our infirmities and understands the need to survive even epic scandals.

Andre Jones walks us through the process of recovery, the power of redemption and the praise that comes with being restored. Read knowing that your life isn't over after a scandal. You can recover.

Bishop Jason Nelson

The Tabernacle at Greater Bethlehem Temple (The Tab)

Randallstown, MD

CONTENTS

INTRODUCTION

I believe that generations choose Christ on their own accord based on the sincerity of the discipler, the efficiency of the gospel and how exactly necessary hearers can resolve forgiveness, grace and eternal life to be for their lives. One terribly unattractive observation is the misconception of how salvation works when we fail to live up to Christ's sacrifice. Many have portrayed sin as an irrevocable termination of redemptive subscription. If that were true, where on earth would we find any redeemed? All blood-washed people have misbehaved at some point, staining themselves.

Does salvation only apply if we can keep it unstained? Is it revocable after repetitious missteps? How many times will God forgive us after the initial pardoning of sin? Has he instructed the church to give us a hard time after repentance? Who reinstates me after I'm forgiven? Do I need a sponsor? These questions are only a fraction of the concerns of present and coming generations who'll decide on Christianity according to the clarity we provide. For this purpose, I've written and shared scenarios in scripture with an explanation of the repentance, restoration and resurgence of the newly forgiven.

Walking with the Lord has been a joy these 20 some years. But if I may be transparent, the only reason I've been so successful at this walk is because I, myself, have recovered. My prayer is that the believers of the 21st century and beyond will know the true and unconventional love of Jesus Christ.

Chapter 1

The Likelihood of Falling

Did you know that failure is not a sovereign superior? Failure does not decide anything as it relates to your fate. While "...the wages of sin is death; but the gift of God is eternal life..."(Rom 6:23 KJV) God, Himself, is the judge, lawyer, and jury in your case. It is the exclusive business of The Almighty to determine where mercy will be applied and who receives the abundance of it. How beautiful is this? God can forgive whatever He wants and whomever He wants, EVEN YOU! Talk about Good News!

AN EXAGGERATION OF SIN'S POWER

Roughly thirty years ago, in the church I grew up in, the prayer line seemed like the "Walk of Shame" for the redeemed. We all stood in a single file line for about an hour and thirty minutes, weeping, and begging to be "RE-saved, then RE-filled". We hadn't yet been taught that our missteps do not cancel out our salvation. Consequently, our flowing tears were the result of being petrified concerning our fate, versus Godly sorrow for where we had failed that week. With fear as a motive for our belief, our tradition was to attend church to beg for mercy.

WHO'S IN THE LINE?

In the prayer line, we have the drunkard who, after receiving his check, disappeared to blow it before the end of the week. By Sunday, now sober, with no money in his pocket, he returns guilty and embarrassed. And that is his motive for "Save me Lawd, Thank ya Geezus" while drooling over a small trash can. No one ever told him, "Sir, you are still redeemed. You are just spiraling out of control due to a crippling habit that you chose to fight alone. The next time you get paid, do not disappear. Come to church!" Isolation was his issue.

I can remember poor Sister Monica walking into service weeping (requiring two missionaries to hold her up) because she had slept with Brother Curtis and felt guilty to the point of being sick in the service. Someone should have said to her, "Excuse me, O Monica, don't you weep and tell Brother Curtis not to moan... anymore. You are currently redeemed. You are lonely and raising children alone, which is even more painful because you look at your incomplete family daily. Bundle up those kids and spend your weekends with some of the married couples. You need moral and spiritual support." I never saw Brother Curtis in the line. I guess he wasn't sorry.

Then there was yours truly. At 10 years old, my mother forced me to get in the prayer line after a conduct notice was sent home from my teacher. I prayed, "Lord help me to do my work in class. Forgive my sins. Help me to stop talking and obey. Amen." I know you meant well, Mom. However, I risked growing up with completely flawed theology. God is not advantageously waiting to punish children and adults for bad behavior. Fortunately, that's not how salvation works! Instead, the Pastor should have whispered in my ear, "Go back and tell your mother to come up here to pray for patience".

All of this because we supposedly stained our salvation in the last week. Ironically, once we were cleansed and forgiven, we instantly became watchmen and failure detectives all over again.

Going to the altar, we only saw how filthy we were. However, on the way back to our seats, we noticed everyone else's dirt. It is the prideful heart of the redeemed. This hypocrisy is the part of Christianity that repels the masses.

THE DEFECTS OF SALVATION

The misconception about salvation is once attained, if you aren't careful, you will consider yourself perfect, foolishly making a pastime of identifying the flaws of others. True worship has proven an anecdote for such Christian arrogance, as it is healthy to balance the pride that comes with being redeemed. When true believers bow at the feet of Jesus, His radiance reminds us all of what we really are without His grace. Without Jesus, we are instantly returned to our natural state, completely flawed and hopelessly doomed: "This I recall to my mind, therefore I have hope. Through the Lord's mercies we are not consumed, because His compassions fail not. They are new every morning: great is Your faithfulness."(Lam 3:21-23 NKJV).

You do remember how Jesus found you, don't you?: "And such were some of you. But you were washed, you were sanctified, you were justified in the name of the Lord Jesus and by the Spirit of our God." (1Cor 6:11 NKJV) This confrontational statement spoken thousands of Christian centuries ago is probably one of the most humbling appeals made to humankind: "SUCH WERE SOME OF YOU"! This scripture brings the mind to recall the journey and means of its present perfection, or should I say redemption, seeing we still aren't flawless. Being redeemed can be so blissful until one forgets ever being saved from anything, even though we were literally acquitted! Paul reminds us of this one paramount truth, no human beings' righteousness is achieved. It's conferred of Christ!

With that said, I'm so glad this book is in your hands. I may be clueless as to why you are reading The Recovery Manual, yet I am one hundred percent confident that this message deserves to, as they say, "go viral"; especially considering not many people make it back from personal condemnation or "peer shame". Recovery is a conversation critical to all humankind because there is a strong possibility you will, one day, find yourself getting up from where you have fallen.

To be honest, I chose Christianity for the recovery benefits; although I personally believe it could stand better advertisement: "Hey! God loved the world so much that He gave His Son for it, and anyone who believes, recovers **forever**!" It would be contradictory to have a redemptive faith short of recovery options. How could life remain sweet or our joy be complete if salvation became null and void the first time we fell short? If that were possible, then why the cross, the nails, or the resurrection?

ALL HAVE SINNED AND ALL WILL SIN

The population of 'mark-missers' is vast and so common that it has become increasingly lucrative and entertaining to report the mistakes of men. It is the way of the world to out one another. But if the entire premise of our faith is that we were eternally doomed and Jesus intervened to His own earthly demise, then the conversation of restoration should be more common. Don't you agree?

So, let's imagine you are recently exposed and everyone knows what you were trying to stop doing before it was too late. **I am asking you to assume the character of the fallen for the**

duration of the book. Those "Lord, forgive me" and "if you give me one more chance" pleas or "I'm going to stop soon" promises to yourself have added up and it seems your grace has expired. You want to fight, run and hide, and expose everyone else you know that has done worse. Unfortunately, believers hardly ever comfort one another in their fallen state. So, I'm ecstatic to be the bearer of such good news! You can recover from this; all is not lost!

THE BIG REVEAL

Even after redeeming you at Calvary, Jesus believes you are worth restoring! But this present exposure is only a necessary prerequisite to finally gain victory over what you have been hiding, that which you were enslaved to. It may be hard to admit that you have been a slave. Paul says, "do you not know that to whom you present yourselves slaves to obey, you are that one's slaves whom you obey, whether of sin leading to death, or of obedience leading to righteousness?" (Rom 6:16 NKJV) You, my friend, thanks to this unforeseen exposure, are no longer a prisoner to the administration of this current scandal; that is, if you have repented.

Now, I know you are thinking, "all that is great, but I am currently scrutinized, mocked, blacklisted, and being slandered. EVERYONE IS DISCUSSING ME!" Unfortunately, your scandal is breaking news to those of us who are religious, who are perfect, who live less eventful lives, or just haven't been featured as of yet.

But today, let's thank God you are finally busted because it is motivation for freedom! You are in a great space!! It may help if you make this your declaration for a while. Come on! Say it! "(insert your name) is in a great space!!" It may be humiliating but it makes great for true repentance. And that is what your life may have lacked - sincere brokenness: "The sacrifices of God are a broken spirit; a broken and a contrite heart- these, O God, you will not despise." (Ps 51:17 NKJV)

WHAT'S YOUR STORY?

I'm sure it's delicate, but let's talk about how you actually got here. Sin, which we can define as contrary behavior to the will, character, and nature of God, isn't so by means of curiosity or negligence alone. Neither are we seduced by any angel turned serpent being coiled up in a tree with a highly intelligent tongue to deceive us, like in Genesis 3. On the contrary! What you have done is accepted the proposition of what appealed to your ***inner desire***. You were distracted.

We knew to do wrong before we honed our preferred vices. It was second nature. This was not something we were introduced to through peer pressure. It is what we discovered to be as innate as our DNA. Truly, it is instinctual and lying dormant until there are laws to break and rules to disregard. Once there is something to lose, here comes the flood. All disobedience needs is an occasion to appeal! Eve didn't eat on a full stomach. She was hungry when the serpent came to her like a waiter at a 5-star restaurant! Personally, I believe curiosity and negligence deserve to be exonerated. SHE WAS HUNGRY! Honestly, I have to admit that these are only administrators of such vices and tendencies, and not to blame altogether.

In King David's prayer of repentance, he admits, "behold, I was shapen in iniquity and in sin did my mother conceive me." (Ps 51:5 KJV) Such transparency forces us to acknowledge just how common sinful behavior really is; so common that it is certain or guaranteed for all.

Dear Reader, you have simply proven *the likelihood of falling*. This does not mean that you do not love the Lord, as much as it proves you have not perfected the degree of discipline that results in unstimulated righteousness. As Paul confirms in 1 Corinthians, we still need help: "So, I do not run aimlessly; I do not box as one beating the air. But I discipline my body and keep it under control, lest after preaching to others I myself should be disqualified." (I Cor 9:26-27 ESV)

I don't mean to harass you with my personal faith, but this is what worked for me. If "...while we were still sinners, Christ died for us" (Rom 5:8 NKJV) is to mean anything, we have got to understand Jesus died for the yet sinning and the inherently sinful who were yet to be born. Jesus is careful in His sacrifice, to bleed enough blood to cover the accident and the incident; the deceived and the seduced. From Eve's curiosity, Adam's hunger, Cain's jealousy, Noah's drunkenness, Moses' striking of the rock, King Saul's disobedience, David's adultery, and even your breaking news, the blood covers! Am I telling you that you are doomed to a life of faultiness, so accept it? God forbid! I'm writing because fallen people are candidates for redemption. The cross was not for your perfection. The old, rugged cross was for your ransom, resulting in justification, vindication, and glorification.

Perhaps you have fallen and were immediately swarmed with cameras, soundbites, memes, blog posts, and social media programs. If your guilt is preserved by viral screenshots or religious whispers of condemnation, this manual is just for you! Let them be, you deserve to breathe life again! You should start taking breaths!

If Jesus believes you are worth dying for; rising from the dead and advocating for you to this very day, I do too! Don't allow shame to harass you out of grace. There is as much redemption as there is sin; love, as there is hate. While there is the likelihood that some will fall, the message of Christ is all the more beautiful; possibly more believable, if you get up! So, get up! When you're ready for the next chapter, please turn the page. It's the only way to go forward!

৵৵৵

Chapter 2

Long Before It Was A Habit

৵৵৵

If you don't experience it, you cannot prefer it!

A MISTAKE. A CHOICE. A CYCLE

Curiosity alone is unable to establish anything as a habit. While fed curiosity can foster obsession, habits are the actual result of satisfied curiosities committed to memory. This is the reason we are instructed to avoid bad energy, resist the devil, shun the very appearance of evil, and have no fellowship with the unbelieving: all biblical directives to prevent an introduction by curiosity.

The impression wrong makes on us is one that happens with eternal intention. What seems harmless is only non-threatening at its inception, because in all actuality, it is playing for keeps! Imagine a welcomed visitor who refuses to leave, that no one can evict.

If, by chance, you have crossed the barrier of curiosity, ponder this question for a moment: Can you recall when it was a mere mistake and not a habit? Often what we mean to do only once serves as the introduction to a life-gripping addiction.

ILL-FOCUSED SANCTIFICATION

I have discovered that iniquity is often the fault of ill-focused sanctification. Let me explain. Biblical standard is how we defend ourselves against falling prey to sinful deeds. The emphasis is too often placed on carrying out the deed versus the desire to do so. I want to suggest a slight glitch in our approach to holiness. The ***standard*** is for the war within, not so much the ***occasion*** where you fall. The war within reveals that a part of you wants to fall. The focus is placed on avoiding the occasion, but the root of the desire is never addressed. A mere occasion only yields time for an already preconceived interest!

I think our rebuke is backwards. Consider this example:

I'm on a date with someone. It's getting heated as everything about the night is perfect. I continuously tell myself not to stay out too late to prevent myself from going too far (guarding against the occasion). Meanwhile, my body is on fire to the point that I've got alternative plans to satisfy my urge once I'm home in bed and alone.

Have you noticed that my desire is accommodated while the occasion for opportunity is rebuked? How many times before desire wins and I indulge in what I strongly crave? Before all of what is currently happening with you took place, what you did was considered harmless because you believed you had it under control. Now, on the exposed end of things, we can agree that "*under control*" and "*under subjection*" are two different things.

LESSOR EVILS AREN'T GOOD ENOUGH

There are always things we ponder that we would love to experience, though we understand they are not too expedient. Either we plead the blood, run the other way and enjoy the mental proximity without the literal indictment or find an alternative evil that is not as wicked as what you would rather not be named among you.

Yes, it is irrefutably true that we love our lesser evils. It is Christianly gratifying to not be as corrupt as the person sitting next to you. Nevertheless, here is the truth. If you could have fellowship with your vice and not be marked by it, some of us would not think twice before indulging. Think about all the things you would do if you could get away with anything. Try not to think too hard, this book is not about dismantling the standard.

PROTECTED BY THE STANDARD

Parenthetically, it is imperative you understand exactly why the standard is even a mandate and conversation amongst believers. Although saved, you are indeed tempted. Yet you are protected as long as the standard of righteousness barricades your life. All of this is for the innate, pending war within and not the occasion where you fall. I have confronted, fought, lost a few times, and eventually, conquered much of this. This is why I am writing this book. I owe it to you to tell you the whole truth.

THE 'OLOGY': BEHAVIOR IS A MANIFESTATION OF BELIEF

There is an "ology" behind everything that we do. In order to get to the root of habit, we must acknowledge our literal thought life (cognitive engine) and just how great the variety of our thoughts are: clean and unclean. Some of everything is conceived in that mind of yours. Your thoughts are cognitive suggestions incubated in the mind until mental and moral negotiation allows them manifestation in personal desire. The process is as follows:

- a thought becomes a desire
- desire apprehends your will
- your will executes your desire
- you feel satisfaction or resentment
- you are met with consequence(s): either good or bad

Here is a scenario:

I am stressed and I need a drink (alcohol justified by emotional exhaustion). After considering the drink, I begin the process of reasoning and rationalizing: I deserve to feel better, right? Now deduction and a slight tug of war take place within because my convictions are against what I honestly want to drink. Eventually, my will comes in harmony with my wants, and soon the glass is filled and tilted to my lips. Now, I am on the opposite side of conviction. "Whew, that was amazing! I overpowered my convictions and was greatly satisfied."

Automatically, the psyche commits the occasion and satisfactory experience to memory in order to suggest it the next time you are stressed. "Just a little drink", you tell yourself, to bypass any guilt. But somehow, after a short while, the inebriation of alcohol lifts and conviction resettles like waves crashing back to the ocean. "What did I just do?" You are resentful as you have broken your criterion. Yet you are deeply satisfied because the drink was all you imagined it to be and it really did mellow things out for a few hours. Remember, stress made it acceptable.

CONSIDER WHAT HAS HAPPENED

I need to show you the probability of wanting/needing a drink again because stress is common in life. What is certain is you *will* consider another drink. You won't deduct, pace the floor, pray or mull over whether it be right or wrong every time. Giving in gets easier once you have dismantled your strong beliefs and ability to refrain, so you will simply pour yourself another glass (side note: this scenario is relevant to all vices).

Laws are our gate and protective barriers, as long as we uphold them. Once righteous convictions are dormant, new norms are welcomed as administrators of habit. You are a new person, like it or not, and such is the case with all behavior contrary to Christian conduct. The non-alcoholic can become an alcoholic, the celibate can become promiscuous, the happily married - horribly adulterous, and the devout steward - a gambler. The journey of becoming "something else", in essence reads like a long story, but honestly, it's a speedy mutation. It doesn't take long at all. "But each one is tempted when he is drawn away by his own desires and enticed. Then, when desire has conceived, it gives birth to sin; and sin, when it is full-grown brings forth death."(James 1:14-15 NKJV) It has happened to the best of us. From a holy bishop to a faithful congregant, we all can admit to the truth of moral decay. But the greatest of error is when we change our ideologies to justify our iniquity. Even if you enjoy the proclivity, you should all the more resent it. It has isolated you, dragged you out of the light into a place of hopelessness, and robbed you of self-control. It will also cost you beautiful fellowship and peace with God.

THE FIRST EXPERIENCE OF RECOVERY IS FORGIVENESS

At this moment, before we go deeper, I want to offer you the strength to resent what has brought you such temporal joy. Long before it was a habit, there was God who was the nucleus of your fulfillment. He is honestly all we have ever needed. Oh to delight in His way again! Would you believe that all it takes is a turn? This means turning to him and turning against what you once chose over him. Throughout history, it has been proven that recovery is best attained through prayers of repentance. The first sign of recovery is God's forgiveness.

David shows us how it's done: "Have mercy on me, O God, according to Your lovingkindness; according to the multitude of Your tender mercies, blot out my transgressions. Wash me thoroughly from my iniquity, and cleanse me from my sin! For I acknowledge my transgressions, and my sin is always before me. Against You, You only, have I sinned and done this evil in your sight - that You may be found just when You speak and blameless when You judge. Behold, I was brought forth in iniquity, and in sin my mother conceived me. Behold, You desire truth in the inward parts, and in the hidden part You will make me to know wisdom. Purge me with hyssop, and I shall be clean; wash me, and I shall be whiter than snow. Make me hear joy and gladness; that the bones You have broken may rejoice. Hide your face from my sins, and blot out all my iniquities. Create in me a clean heart, O God, and renew a steadfast spirit within me. Do not cast me away from Your presence, and take not your Holy Spirit from me. Restore to me the joy of Your salvation and uphold me by Your generous spirit. Then I will teach transgressors Your ways, and sinners shall be converted to You:" (Ps 51:1-13 NKJV)

If I told you that you could recover your life before convictions were forfeited or broken, what would you do? Whatever that is, start doing it now! "Therefore, if anyone is in Christ, he is a new creation; old things have passed away; behold, all things have become new." (2 Cor 5:17 NKJV) This scripture is often mistaken as a defense against indictment. However, you will definitely be held responsible and have to address the effects of what you've done, especially if it altered the lives of people. Contrary to popular belief, a redeemed man or woman can outlive an aging tale any day. Every time there's a reference made to what you did, it's humiliated by how much you've changed. New will always cause resentment, dismissal, and expiration to that which is old.

ঌঌঌ

Chapter 3

Lord Forgive Me, Again

ঌঌঌ

Willpower isn't enough power. Don't fool yourself.

HABITUAL PSYCHOLOGY

Have you ever attempted to convince yourself that you're stronger than your temptation? You'll say things like: "I'm not gonna do it! Well, maybe I won't do too much so I can say I haven't totally fallen" or "I just need a little bit more to relax my mind. Okay, I'm gonna stop before it's too late because I love this feeling but loathe the guilt." Then after a few minutes, you conclude: "I've come this far, I may as well finish. Lord, please forgive me...AGAIN!"

Isn't it funny how often we repent for the same exact thing? Our faultiness, or liability, has very little to do with the habitual, preferred sins that we attribute to mere learning experiences. Did you know that minimizing an offense takes away from the true power of conviction? If falling is necessary as a means to learning, our repentance record should consist of a variety of faults, justified with an equal amount of lessons; not the same misstep! How many times do you take the same course?

A repeat offender thinks like this, "if they would just change the rules, we wouldn't have to go through the tiresome process of being arrested, charged, tried, convicted, and sentenced." The iniquitous mind believes the process and policies to be merciless, unreasonable, and unnecessary. The process and policies are believed to be the actual problem more than the crime itself. They will blame the system before they regret their behavior. To them, the circumstances justify the crime, which is why they continue their habitual pattern.

Let's look closer. A drug user will subscribe to their choice of drug as long as their problems suggest. An adulterer will live a double life to cope with the obligation of the life he or she hates. The thief will steal every time they're met with the crisis of not having enough resources. Friends, these are the coping behaviors of those who aren't impressed to change, although they are made miserable by their ever-present conditions. Their solution is to change the rules since they can't change their circumstances.

If you notice, very little attention is given to the breaking of moral, ethical, and spiritual laws that make life simple. We have to believe that God's way is perfect without fault. It's not only lawful, it's expedient: "therefore you shall keep every commandment which I command you today, that you may be strong, and go in and possess the land which you cross over to possess, and that you may prolong your days in the land which the Lord swore to give your fathers, to them and their descendants, 'a land flowing with milk and honey.' " (Deut 11:8-9 NKJV) Unfortunately, when shy of regret, an apology is all a transgressor can offer.

THE GRIEF SYNDROME

Repentance, without rededication and the courage to denounce the vice, is only a means to withstanding temporary guilt. If you do not change what you believe about the criticality of your shortcomings, what you ought to say is, "Lord, excuse me!" Once memory logs an experience into the cerebral file, the incentive will rise again and the said deed is justified in a flicker of a second. As a repeat offender, you are dependent on whatever the particular proclivity provides as a supplement.

This "hole in the soul" epidemic is known to facilitate many candidates in search of fulfillment. I don't believe you are completely evil. On the contrary, you are continuously penitent and are still in the fold. You didn't choose to leave the faith altogether. Coming to church isn't the easiest thing to do when you are dragging guilt. In today's society, many simply unsubscribe from the faith to have peace in error. Truth is, if you don't believe in the standard of righteousness, you won't feel as if you've missed any necessary mark. The mark then becomes an irrelevant standard.

YOU STILL HAVE A HEART

At least you still believe it's wrong. You just haven't figured out how to fill or heal the void. It's safe to admit that there's something partially fulfilling about the transgression. We'll need to agree that every law and admonition given to the believer in scripture is in consideration of God's own perfection: "All Scripture is given by inspiration of God, and is profitable for doctrine, for reproof, for correction, for instruction in righteousness, that the man of God may be complete, thoroughly equipped for every good work." (2 Tim 3:16-17 NKJV) So "thou shalt not", is actually the "how-to curriculum" of mortal perfection. In other words, if you mind the "shall nots", you'll come out Christlike. Peter admonishes us "...as he who called you is holy, you also be holy in all your conduct..." (1 Peter 1:15-16 ESV) With this being true, our choice of iniquity or missing of the mark, being minimized and discounted as a matter of mere perspective and not the severe offense that it is, is a literal attack on God's divine perfection.

DON'T REPENT FOR MANNERS

True repentance requires resentment of the deceiver, regret for the deed, a renouncing of the ideology that justified the sin, and a swift returning to God; the true filler of all human void. While the mercies of God endure forever, to spend a lifetime repenting is to never live out His amazing plan for your life! This time when we repent, we are going to turn, run the other way, and live! Even if we've got to run through critical crowds and those who don't quite sin as well as we do.

Pray with me:

Dear Lord, today we confess true sorrow for our transgressions. What worthless affairs we've committed! This open apology isn't a matter of Christian manners to shake the misery of conviction. Avoiding guilt and shame doesn't secure freedom or deliverance. Savior, only you can restore us to liberty and give us residency in your presence again. So to You, we appeal. Cleanse us whole! In Jesus name, Amen

Chapter 4

As Long As It Was a Secret

How do you like your repentance; public or private?

PRIVATE REPENTANCE vs PUBLIC EXPOSURE

Do you remember having to go before the church when you messed up? Didn't it seem like we were waiting to be forgiven by the people? This "walk of shame" was more damaging than the guilt before God Himself. Ever wonder why? I have learned with spiritual maturity that it takes both God and humbling transparency to stay free indeed.

One of the best features of repentance is that it's an appeal to Heaven and not a confession amongst peers. We don't need a priest. Our High Priest is ever-present. Fortunately, you can cry to God anywhere: at the altar, in your car, with your pastor, by yourself. It can be on a Sunday or the very second you've come to your senses. But, if you're not careful, you will never really change because the only true repellent to darkness is unrestricted light. And for some, private penitence only clears the conscience, without disarming the stronghold of its possession. A casual, off the record, "Lord, forgive me" never delivered anyone!

In other words, repenting in private simply spares us the experience we fear most: utter embarrassment. The public exposure of our unfaithfulness to God and the truth of our consecutively missing the standard we've subscribed to, are two different extremes. It's true, we'd rather only God know that we struggle or dabble. If our colleagues knew, the shame would eat away at our ego and more than likely would take longer to recover. Why? Peers don't forget and they often keep score.

Consequently, we develop a higher tolerance for guilt (personal judgment) while having an allergic reaction to shame (the public's condemnation). God's unending grace, seemingly without consequence, is much more delightful than a mortal judge and jury.

AN ACTUAL LOOK AT YOUR SCENARIO

Sometimes we see best in retrospect, so I'd like to take a few moments to observe things from a reflective point of view. Before the flood of phone calls, screenshots, side meetings, text messages, and the utter shock of things growing beyond your management, can you remember what was most important to you? More than likely it wasn't deliverance, because the habitual nature had already set in. Once we're imprisoned within the cycle, we tend to become compliant with the idea that what we're doing is either right or impossible to resist. By this time, we've fallen into hopelessness and the lifestyle of portrayal. Portrayal? Absolutely! Meanwhile, under sin's spell, you are still a part of a people group, the religious circle that prides itself not only on its redemption and salvation but more importantly, sanctification to the extreme of perfection. In other words, holiness is right!

We've all heard the popular testimonies: "I looked at my hands and they looked new, looked at my feet and they did too!" or "Things I used to do, I don't do no more. Places I used to go, I don't go no more!" I think you get it by now...

Much of our Christian esteem is the practice of being sanctimonious: the outward display of inner perfection. Therefore, we are careful never to indicate that our darkened humanity is alive and well. Here's the truth: When you're caught up in the habit of your preferred joy and decide to believe that what you're doing is either right or necessary, you're still a religious soul. Therefore, you'll resolve that as long as it's a secret, all is well. You yield yourself to a life of deception instead of crying out for help. Don't settle for the secret: "Confess your trespasses to one another, and pray for one another, that you may be healed. The effective, fervent prayer of a righteous man avails much." (James 5:16 NKJV)

You will find yourself working tirelessly to acquire a means to achieving a successful double lifestyle if you don't confess your struggle. It sounds something like this: keeping breath spray or gum and a change of clothes in the car, erasing your search history, spraying cologne before entering a religious setting, staying in an undisclosed location to fortify your privacy, keeping other people's scandal at hand to avoid blackmail, throwing away receipts, buying gifts for silence and, possibly, spending more money than you truly have in order to satisfy those who know too much (affairs get expensive), always requiring excessive pledges of loyalty from your circle, playing mind games, using manipulation and so much more. All this to guarantee entry and comfortability amongst those who subscribe to sanctification and are of like precious faith. This, my friend, is a common Christian epidemic. The believer's image is sometimes literally all there is left to see.

A KING BY CHARGE - AN ADULTERER BY CHOICE

"It happened in the spring of the year, at the time when kings go out to battle, that David sent Joab, and his servants with him, and all Israel; and they destroyed the people of Ammon and besieged Rabbah. But David remained in Jerusalem. Then it happened one evening that David arose from his bed and walked on the roof of the king's house. And from the roof, he saw a woman bathing, and the woman was very beautiful to behold. So David sent and inquired about the woman. And someone said, 'Is this not Bathsheba, the daughter of Eliam, the wife of Uriah the Hittite?' Then David sent messengers and took her, and she came to him, and he lay with her, for she was cleansed from her impurity; and she returned to her house. And the woman conceived; so she sent and told David, and said, 'I am with child.' " (2 Sam 11:1-5 NKJV)

David, an appointed king established by God himself, was literally God's choice among men. He was a worshiper and a warrior whose responsibility was to lead Israel in war, especially during the spring. You'd lose your life if you addressed King David with any less adoration and reverence because his worth and ego hinged on how he was seen and regarded - as a King! But have you noticed in the text that he's not doing anything he's called to do?

We are creatures who prioritize imagery, at any cost, over authenticity. As long as no one knows our faultiness, we are perfectly content with looking the part: Address me as a worshiper, though I've not bowed my head. Revere me as a shepherd, while I fleece the sheep. Honor me as God's vessel, though I'm in a backslidden state. Yet, we require that our identities are acknowledged even if we're unfaithful to our own charge.

"In the morning it happened that David wrote a letter to Joab and sent it by the hand of Uriah. And he wrote in the letter, saying, 'Set Uriah in the forefront of the hottest battle, and retreat from him, that he may be struck down and die.' " (2 Sam 11:14-15 NKJV)

David would extinguish a life to save his own image. My question to you: Are you this image-driven that you'd leave us with your perfectly religious hologram? Or will you admit that you need God's grace and are grateful that He's not denied you of it?

Let the secret out! You've done some horrible things that only open exposure could help you overcome. Now, you are free and don't care who knows it. There's nothing left after repentance but **restoration**! "Let the wicked forsake his way, and the unrighteous man his thoughts; let him return to the Lord, and he will have mercy on him, and to our God, for he will abundantly pardon." (Isaiah 55:7 NKJV)

If you want freedom, tell your secrets. It will initially sting, but it's a beautiful pain when it makes you free.

ঌ৯ঌ৯ঌ৯

Chapter 5

Beautifully Busted

ঌ৯ঌ৯ঌ৯

When Christians are exposed, it's actually God taking them back from the enemy's deception. He's saying, "They are mine, that's as far as you're taking them!" Believe me when I say, being busted isn't the worst thing in the world. It's a bridge to grace and restoration.

DIDN'T SEE IT COMING

God wants you back on destiny's path: "Let us search out and examine our ways, and turn back to the Lord; Let us lift our hearts and hands to God in heaven." (Lam 3:40-41 NKJV) The gasps for air, dizziness, pounding heart, soaring blood pressure and the feeling of nakedness that comes from unforeseen exposure are indescribable, to say the least. There is no worse confrontation than the one you don't suspect; when you don't even see it coming. It's like the shock of being shot and not knowing where. All you are sure of is you're hit. It's always an ambush so impactful that you don't have time to fake being unbothered, be quick on your feet, or portray confidence. There's no time to give counter statements and alternative facts! You are completely humiliated and most emotional because you've worked so faithfully to live a successful double lifestyle. Revelation 3: 15-16 (NKJV) warns us that a double lifestyle is dangerous: "I know your works, that you are neither cold nor hot: I could wish you were cold or hot. So then, because you are lukewarm, and neither cold nor hot, I will vomit you out of My mouth"

However, the person who leaked your story, sent your screenshots, called around on you, betrayed your very vulnerable trust, humiliated you, and caused pain like you've never felt in all your days is not to blame! No one person or group has enough power to expose what grace has once covered. The love of God is behind all of this. When God wants you back in destiny's path, He'll release what seems like bloodhounds of rescue and restoration after you and they'll incur any cost to bring you home.

- Home to your once discarded convictions.
- Home to confession and repentance.
- Home to genuine worship and fellowship.
- Home to his arms and your sober self.

"For the Lord your God is a consuming fire, a jealous God." (Deut 4:24 NKJV)

THINGS ARE COMING BACK TO NORMAL

To the natural eye, it looks as if your life is coming apart at the seams. Actually, it's coming back together. We all have a sanctioned distance to wander, but after a while, our Father calls us in. When we're precious to God, but at home in our sin, God will practically stop time to reconstruct our path.

Since we left off with King David in the previous chapter, let's continue observing this high-profile scandal. Nathan said to David, "...You are the man! Thus says the Lord, the God of Israel, 'I anointed you king over Israel, and I delivered you out of the hand of Saul. I gave you your master's house and your master's wives into your keeping and gave you the house of Israel and Judah. And if that had been too little, I also would have given you much more! Why have you despised the commandment of the Lord, to do evil in his sight? You have killed Uriah the Hittite with the sword; you have taken his wife to be your wife and have killed him with the sword of the people of Ammon.' " (2 Sam 12:7-9 ESV)

GOD'S MERCY AT WORK

Remember having all your ducks in a row? Your story was prepped, disposition perfected, all while going about your daily life. As a pastor, I teach my church that the anointed always get caught. The moment that deadening text, screenshot, or phone call comes, you have to decide what you care about the most: Will you fight this? Will you run and hide? Should you hire a publicist, a hitman, or just own it?

It's called retreating to conjure your story or strategy. However, lying is such a taxing resolve because the truth just won't cooperate with the lies. Almost immediately, you deactivate your social media pages. Your automated receptionist (voicemail) takes all your calls. Church is the last place you want to go, and your friends and family have to form search parties to be sure you're ok! Oftentimes, you're blind-sided so it's impossible to know who exactly to trust. Is this the judgment of God informing that your grace is depleted or is it the hatred of your enemies who plotted against you and you didn't see it coming? You really don't know what to think on day one of being BUSTED!

The more popular, logical thought is God's wrath is upon me. You instantly recall those, "Lord, if you forgive me, I'll never do it again" prayers. How many more times did you do it again and again and again? It's too late to hide, yet a fine time to confess. The trauma of being exposed tends to cloud our ability to see God's mercy at work. In the David and Bathsheba narrative, it was a year later before the Prophet Nathan was sent to confront King David. It wasn't until after this that David repented. You ask the question, what did King David do for an entire year? The same thing you've been doing; ***covering*** and ***convening***, as you do so well.

"So David said to Nathan, 'I have sinned against the Lord.' And Nathan said to David, 'The Lord also has put away your sin; you shall not die'."(2 Sam 12:13 NKJV) For as long as you lived in deception, there was a barrier between you and God, because your image became your idol. This is the reason you could offend almighty God, but privately repent, while maintaining your righteous image and then sin against God all over again. Sometimes on repeat. Being exposed is being rescued from the cycle of falling. It's not until it all comes out that you can resent, regret, reconcile and sincerely return to the Lord.

Secrets are like debt. They maintain access to any season of your life until they are rectified and resolved. I believe God is after his investment. It isn't your grace that has expired, but rather his tolerance for such a season. It's time you know who you're called to be. "For whom the Lord loves He chastens, and scourges every son whom He receives. If you endure chastening, God deals with you as with sons; for what son is there whom a father does not chasten? But if you are without chastening, of which all have become partakers, then you are illegitimate and not sons." (Heb 12:6-8

NKJV) Being busted is likened unto friends breaking you out of an island jail where there aren't any landlines, cell phone towers, fire for a smoke signal, or hope of ever getting free. Just be glad you've been found!

Chapter 6

It Just Went Viral

Not my kind of fame

IT'S OUT THERE NOW

It's Wednesday and you get off work early. Before pulling out of the parking lot, you ask yourself, "Should I go straight to church or go home for a little while?" You decide to head in the direction of the church and be early for midweek service. Jokingly, as you pull up to the church, you say, "For once in my life, I'll be on time!" You walk into church, and surprisingly, all eyes are on you. You have no clue that the stares and the whispers are about you. You head to the restroom to check your appearance and hear your name in the stalls. At that very second, your phone repeatedly buzzes as if you have been without service for a while and just regained a signal.

Something is definitely wrong...

The phrase "I just went viral" is celebratory for some, yet reason for suicide in the case of others. Nonetheless, we gloat in the greatest communicative breakthrough of our time, which is, social media. Technology is the patented solution to a problem that can sustain itself into the future. Its present use is essential until rising generations, gifted with the instinct of improvement, build upon its foundation. It's all about improvement.

Technology is also a baton passed to further revolutionize time. Even communication itself looks and functions differently from the telephone's first use over a century ago. In the 1980s, Motorola introduced the pager, aka the beeper, cornering the communication market with absolute genius. That's until the cellphone availed us the ability to text, leaving us no need for the trendy multicolored box hanging from our belts. We have evolved from standing in one spot while talking, to running errands or even taking a jog while communicating. From beepers to mobile phones, smartphones to smartwatches, the creative solves problems that provide upcoming generations a foundation to build upon, creating greater conveniences for their era. But unfortunately, these conveniences can sometimes backfire. Do they backfire due to malfunction or because they are mishandled? Who is to blame?

THE INTERNET

I don't believe Sir Tim Berners-Lee was burdened with fostering an efficient means for slander when he created the world wide web in 1989. I'm almost certain he did not acquire any interest at all in something so baseless. How to gossip was not an issue plaguing early America. No, the internet wasn't exactly created for scandal, but like anything in the earth, it stands to be perverted. It's also rather interesting to see the old proverb ring true even in the cyberspace age, "bad news travels quicker than good news" and I would like to add if good news travels at all! The worldwide system of networks created for the expansion of communication isn't at all substantiated by the sinister nature of gossipers and tea drinkers. No, the internet is not to blame.

THE INTERNET IS TAKEN CAPTIVE

It's not the internet causing such havoc. On the contrary, the internet, I believe, was an answer to the technological concerns of our evolving century. Mass communication, machinery, electronic payments, the keeping of records, the cataloging of information to be at the fingertips of the common man, and much more innovation is possible because of this technological breakthrough. We must remember that the human will, intent, motive, conviction, or lack thereof, lies behind the use of all machinery. There are a few personality traits that God literally hates: "a proud look, a lying tongue, hands that shed innocent blood, a heart that devises wicked plans, feet that are swift in running to evil, a false witness who speaks lies, and one who sows discord among brethren" to name a few (Prov 6:16-19 NKJV).

A MATTER OF MORAL CONSCIENCE

Moral conscience is always in charge of the human will, and many with a camera phone, iPad, and social media account, do not have one at all. So, the epidemic of unnecessary captures and inappropriate footage is becoming common to our personal pocket screens. If you pull out your phone right now and log on to one of your social media accounts, you will be met with several posts that are useless and unnecessary; yet for some, entertaining. It is the corrupt mind of men and women that desire to visually reproduce and draw others to their personal perspectives and views. They do not often consider how their followers will feel about their status, picture, or video. Those who post, post what is important to them.

It is a clear revelation of their passion, interest, and mentality. So, imagine the darkened heart and mind of the individual who posts, reposts, broadcasts, group chats, and screenshots scandal, especially the religious type. Clearly, the content is of no use to the Lord's church. To be found a connoisseur of such gruesome references and play-by-play details of people's misfortune is a character flaw. But mischief has a page just like the rest of us.

To the featured personnel, I am not excited about your untimely debut, neither am I entertained. Unfortunately, you fall to the mercy of every person with a computer and a page. It's a shame no one checks the state of our viral de-sensations. Is anyone concerned about whether or not you are alone while your world crumbles? Is there just not enough entertainment on TV these days? Can all the parties involved stand to relive the past every single time you are referenced online? Maybe some are guilty as charged, but at what point do we do unto others as we would have them do unto us?

To those of you who have the testimony "I just went viral" and have been affected as society has taken your misstep, mishap, accusation, or fall as cheap entertainment, I do apologize. Not everyone gone viral is guilty and not every guilty party deserves to be social media famous. Death to needless commentary that leaves no possibility of life after exposure!

Chapter 7

Darn Bloggers and Joggers

Sometimes it's not a matter of good or bad, just motive.

'WHY' IS THE MATTER WITH YOU?

We can all agree that high school is too impressionable of a time in life not to make the social cut. Lorenzo Valdez wasn't the football player or prom king kind of guy. In fact, he was ignored by the entire class of 1998. Unfortunately, Lorenzo didn't fit into a memorable class or group of people. He was ignored for four whole years! Being unseen made him wish all the more to be treated like those whom everyone else admired.

By the 20-year class reunion, all who were esteemed had dwindled down to a most average existence. They had gained weight, aged horribly, and were working average jobs. In short, they just weren't exactly 'to die for' anymore. However, Valdez was the CEO of a Fortune 500 company, drove a Mercedes 750, and was married to a fashion model. They had a handsome son and owned 3 homes in different states. Life had been pretty good to him.

Being a "nobody" in high school was the motivation for Valdez's drive and self-commitment to achieve a wonderful life. With his success, he does more than just attend the reunion. Valdez pays the entire bill. With the simple swipe of a black card, he forced his classmates to acknowledge how successful he had become. Valdez emphasized how the mighty (the popular) had plateaued in the most self-aggrandizing way. His actions describe personal vindication perfectly. Anyone who thinks for one moment that he funded the class reunion out of kindness is sadly mistaken. Valdez did a beautiful thing from a vengeful heart!

PSYCHOLOGY OF A VENDETTA JOURNALIST

The true root of scandal blogging comes from the experience of being ignored (like Valdez) at some point in life. We have to differentiate and wedge separation between justice and vengeance to completely understand the complex heart of the person who stands for right, versus the one who gains a sense of relevance (which they've never attained) by making a name off of another's misfortune.

The blogger introduces themselves as the champion for

right. They aim to incite accountability for wrongdoing and justice for the underdog. Over time, fear of the scandal blogger becomes widespread. It breeds compliance in the form of attention, deference, friendship, accouterment, and devout pledges of loyalty and allegiance that turn such a person's heart inside out. The ability to provoke such cooperation results in a pseudo power. Though it's love, by way of fear, the Valdezes of the world gladly accept such devotion as pure and authentic.

That is what power does in the hands of the vengeful. What scandal blogger have you seen that doesn't want revenge from a people group, peer group, or organization? Yes, if we behave no one will have anything to report but that's not the focus of this book. Have you considered the psychological state of the ingenious, self-made news anchor?

MUTATION OF HEART TO STONE

Consequently, the lamb becomes a lion who thrives off the entire forest scattering when they strut through. This is quite common in the "I've Never Been Regarded" narrative. A scorned woman or a broken man venting through a platform (masked in religious passion) amounts to nothing but life-altering gossip coined as breaking news; all to the glory of the talebearer. The Scandal Blogger is not to be praised as a humanitarian. It was receptivity that made the "media-tell-all" industry a thing. The joggers, as I like to call those who run steadily to subscribe to our 21st-century tattlers, avail them jaw-dropping ratings to build their own personal empires, destroying lives in the process... all with the click of a button.

Whenever we gain attention, intentionally or not, we stop at nothing to keep it. Who can argue that mass Christendom is hypnotized and firmly subscribed with bulging inboxes and exhausted gigabytes of breaking news? It is difficult to run with purpose and specialize in other people's affairs at the same time. But when you have no personal business, it gives you a dose of optimism to try anything. If the joggers would commit to their own lives, the bloggers would find themselves about as revered as the nosy old lady who sits in the window. She sees all, but she isn't an industry or enterprise. She is just a plain ol' retired lady with time on her hands. No one calls her a savior for knowing everyone's business.

Lorenzo Valdez is a common case of getting even with life through masked intentions. It's true, sometimes it's not a matter of good or bad, just motive.

❧❧❧

Chapter 8

Steps to Recovery

❧❧❧

At some point, if we don't call our children out of the corner and off punishment, they'll miss out on the ordained ministry of the family!

IT'S TIME WE REINSTATE THE FALLEN

The truth is, no one can stay in a single circumstance forever lest they die. Time will proceed forward whether it's dragging us along or memorializing us with heartfelt condolences because we gave up and stopped living. Have you ever stopped to think about the true meaning of Christianity? Its very nature is redemption! Exposure is an epidemic while recovery is hardly a trend. Imagine a redeeming faith with no recovery plan should you fall? A poorly thought-out concept, right? Aren't you glad God authored your salvation glitch-free? There's hope for the sinner and even the sinning saint!

With this in mind, it's very much imperative that we consider a very controversial truth to live free of pending condemnation. If God didn't kill us in our error, we're undoubtedly preserved for a new era! Therefore, own the grace and mercy of God given to you. It is time to fathom 'life after scandal' because the body of Christ is purposed to refresh and heal itself; even as the natural body recovers strength in time. To stay in the house, reject phone calls, avoid loved ones, and watch movies all day while eating massive salad bowls of cereal is, in essence, falling off the face of the earth. I'll bet that's a sin too! The question is, do you have the gumption to live beyond the ambush and return to your purpose - the actual reason you are here?

Now, I'm sure in many cases we've been left to manage on our own because self-righteous people find it necessary to cease fellowship with those overtaken in a fault. What we as Christians may not theoretically comprehend is the actual body lends all of its strength and attention to the detrimental, yet wounded area. We are to surround the fallen believer with love and prayers lest Satan completely plucks them out of the faith with depression, shame, brokenness, loneliness, and injured pride, which were all caused by the response of their supposed brothers and sisters.

Paul advised the first century church against circumstantial unity: "And if one member suffers, all the members suffer with it; or if one member is honored, all the members rejoice with it. Now you are the body of Christ, and members individually." (1 Cor 12:26-27

NKJV) Unfortunately, in today's time, it's more like the hand saying to the arm, "Did you hear what happened to the foot? Glad it wasn't me!" Instead of yielding empathy and sincere concern to console a valuable yet broken counterpart, we gloat that it is not us. According to Galatians 6:1(NKJV), this response is contrary to our faith: "Brethren, if a man is overtaken in any trespass, you who are spiritual restore such a one in a spirit of gentleness, considering yourself, lest you also be tempted."

The restoration we speak of is an activity and behavior from an organism that understands it is incomplete without the fallen or wounded person being made whole. Too often we leave people to wait it out with advice like, "It'll blow over", which doesn't require much sincerity. I truly apologize for this character flaw and fruit of the spirit scarcity. Whether officially restored or eventually you return, there is a way to find your place in your particular society again.

THE RECOVERY PROCESS

In the worst-case scenario, if no one comes to your rescue and you are left to recover alone, here are a few things to consider that will help you cope with those swift transitions and find your way back to normalcy. Realize that it's by the grace of God that you are alive to be found out. Though guilt and shame are relentless in their plight to show no mercy while ferociously pulling you apart, God is actually on your side.

- **Acknowledge that you messed up.**
  "...for all have sinned and fall short of the glory of God..." (Rom 3:23 NKJV) You, my dear friend, are not the first to make the "Christian News" and it's rather safe to say you won't be the last. Nevertheless, we can responsibly leave a trail for the next person who will need a sure path back to freedom. A scandal, if not survived, eats your bright future and vehemently flushes it down the toilet. So I need you to listen closely because you still matter. You cannot die here! Although it may sound like a great idea to avoid the embarrassment, you must keep going.

- **Quickly inform your leaders.**
  Considering that you may not have been in counsel for deliverance or practicing accountability before now, you should be the first to tell them. Don't allow them to be ambushed, having to account for what they didn't know. It's not a matter of your story bringing shame on your church or denomination as much as the fact that there is a current spiritual battle for your soul. If you are under a covering, you have a right to be covered and protected, especially at this time. Your spiritual authority will be spirit-led in guarding and restoring you properly. "And I will give you shepherds

according to My heart, who will feed you with knowledge and understanding." (Jer 3:15 NKJV)

- **Stop talking about it.**

  Pride and ego make you create false stories, deduct from the truth, and double back. You are willing to fight against all of social media to salvage your image. If all God sees is you fighting for your own honor, He can't see your contrite heart and broken spirit (Ps 51:17 NKJV). If what you've done has hurt innocent people, concern yourself with them and not so much the masses, the memes, and social media commentary.

- **Live one day at a time.**

  Remember that all timelines move 90 miles per hour daily. Surely, you won't trend forever. This is reason enough to retire from your media watchtower and attend to your everyday life and responsibilities. Consider that if your story isn't a crime resulting in you being charged and sentenced, the only misery you'll suffer is criticism. Again, this will not last forever. Social media timelines force us along with breaking news by the second. There is no sense in you behaving like this single moment is the climax of your life. Be still and take it one day at a time.

- **Surround yourself with trusted friends and family to**

avoid a breakdown from the pressure.

It is imperative that you are not alone, but you will need more than just company. Your circumstances demand people who are a balm and healing presence to your heart and mind. I'm not too sure that this is a job for new friends. If I were you, I would reach for my tenured group. More than likely, they can handle you and anything that comes in your direction. "A friend loves at all times, and a brother is born for adversity." (Prov 17:17 NKJV)

- **Beware of those who pretend to care about you and your situation.**

Within a peer group, there are commonly two positions to be mindful of. One, the informant who will report to you everything "they" are saying which is what you do not need to hear. The other is the leak. The leak positions themselves to know all and communicates with the outside circles about inside details. For instance, "Yeah, we had to go get Keisha off the bridge, she was about to kill herself!" To boost their value, they'll sell your most critical moments which in turn creates a snowball of commentary for bloggers and joggers.

- **Begin to thank God for your new beginning!**

Although it is birthed from demolition, it is the way out of the iniquity you couldn't break away from. Because you were enjoying whatever you were doing, it made it difficult to quit. I am sure you can admit, it didn't hurt to do it, but getting caught did. God's quiet mercy doesn't often convict us out of our transgression. God saw the whole thing and you knew that. This exposure is step one to your deliverance. Yes, being exposed is a direct attack on your ego, but a small price for freedom.

- **Let shame fade away.**

  If you've truly repented, guilt is absorbed. Don't fight accusers due to your embarrassment. Here is the truth, it's everyone's present but your past. "There is therefore now no condemnation to those who are in Christ Jesus, who do not walk according to the flesh, but according to the Spirit." (Rom 8:1 NKJV) Prayerfully, you've long changed your walk!

- **Respect God's grace and be humbled by the experience.**

  Arrogance will make you say, "I'm still here", "The devil thought he had me", "People try to tear you down", "I'm still anointed", "Y'all doing mess too", or "It made me stronger!" None of that defensive garbage will save your soul. Only brokenness. You threw yourself on the mercy of God's court. Please do not get up from the altar arrogant. Your life now belongs to God who is rich in mercy. Pay your debt with thanksgiving and come back praising. "What shall

I render to the Lord for all His benefits toward me? I will take the cup of salvation, and call upon the name of the Lord. I will pay my vows to the Lord now in the presence of all His people." (Ps 116:12-14 NKJV)

- **Resurface with power over what once tripped you up**. The relevance of your entire ordeal was that you obtained power over what you once could not contend against. Jesus getting power over death, hell, and the grave meant first dying, going to hell, and literally rising from a grave assigned to him forever. When He arose, He rose never to die again. You ought to never be a victim to this stronghold ever again. Rise with victory. "Therefore God also has highly exalted Him, and given Him the name which is above every name, that at the name of Jesus every knee should bow, of those in heaven, and of those on earth, and of those under the earth, and that every tongue should confess that Jesus Christ is Lord, to the glory of God the Father." (Phil 2:9-11 NKJV) When your name perseveres, power is the reward. You are no longer just the person who fell. You are now 'the revered who rose'. Something has happened to your name.

  Something so great, it's now above scandal's reach!

ॐॐॐ

Chapter 9

Recovery and Resurfacing

ॐॐॐ

Lifestyle changes aren't easy at all, especially when you aren't convinced that they are necessary.

DON'T IGNORE THE SIGNS

In many cases, drastic changes are only embraced through problematic circumstances. Aware of the risk and repercussions of our habits, we are optimistic to believe that fate and reciprocity will show respect of person to us. Talk about the misapplication of faith. Nevertheless, the old faithful traumatic experience wins time and time again. It tends to be the greatest catalyst to expedite such procrastinated change. It never fails.

Give a man a locked engine and he'll decide to take better care of the vehicle that daily transports his family and gets him back and forth to work. But long before the engine locked, there was the check engine light that was faithful to give fair warning. Unfortunately, we ignore the courtesy of signs every day. It's astonishing to observe us know better but not do better until we are forced to. Something has to be on the line for a man to alter his own course.

YOU ARE NOT THE ACCUSATION

So you ignored the signs. The engine locked but you've been blessed with a new car. My question to you as you proceed forward, who are you? The answer to this simple, yet profound question will determine how you live your life beyond this point. Now, remember, you are not what you did. You are not the accusation. The bloggers aren't interested enough in you to keep up with your maturation and evolution. Consequently, their stories are dated. It's not their priority to present you to the public again. By this chapter of The Recovery Manual, it's safe to say you've survived the inception, threat, and traumatic shock of your story. You are now ready to grow from it all. Who have you become? This question must be answered after your experience.

You are now the person that will walk into rooms and when it gets quiet, you will be comfortable knowing that the poor souls whispering and texting do not know who you are! You are the person who simply appreciates being a better person and a brand new creature. "Therefore, if anyone is in Christ, he is a new creation: old things have passed away; behold, all things have become new." (2 Cor 5:17 NKJV) You are the person who values God's mercy; the temporal shame amongst peers and colleagues means very little. You have made peace with all parties involved in said scandal and understand that reinstatement is the lot of all public offense.

WHEN MERCY LEAVES YOU ALIVE

After God's grace falls over you, you can return to society with pride and dignity to kill your legend. Consider David's restoration account in scripture. All of Israel and its leadership were engulfed in the David and Bathsheba scandal. The Prophet Nathan had come and gone, serving God's rebuke and fitting sentence. David fasted for a week praying for the healing of his infant child, the spawn of his affair. The temple servants stood back, collectively watching the king wrestle to maintain his sanity when the child died. Observe David's response, "so David arose from the ground, washed and anointed himself, and changed his clothes; and he went into the house of the Lord, and worshipped. Then he came to his own house; and when he requested, they set food before him, and he ate." (2 Sam 12:20 NKJV) When the child died, King David realized that mercy left him alive. What do you do when mercy and the blood of Jesus win your case? It's not a difficult question at all, you rise in the glory of His love and return to your life. By all means, what publication does the grace of God receive if you never resurface?

Let's also consider a female in the scriptures who was pardoned and reinstated. This woman was caught in the act. She couldn't deny the accusation. Look at Jesus' response and His instruction to the adulteress, post forgiveness. "So when they continued asking Him, He raised Himself up and said to them, 'He who is without sin among you, let him throw a stone at her first.' And again he stooped down, and wrote on the ground. Then those who heard it, being convicted by their conscience, went out one by one, beginning with the oldest even to the last. And Jesus was left alone, and the woman standing in the midst. When Jesus had raised Himself up, and saw no one but the woman, He said to her, 'Woman, where are those accusers of yours? Has no one condemned you?' She said, 'No one, Lord.' And Jesus said to her, 'Neither do I condemn you: go and sin no more.' " (John 8: 7-11 NKJV)

You aren't only forgiven, you are dismissed! Go, and sin no more. Your value is what God invested in you that He counted worthy of saving. It is imperative that you return to the very place of accusation, indictment, and ridicule to be found whole and on another wise. It is easy to follow Jesus to another region, state, city, new church, or peer group, but you are indeed a much more impactful testimony showing up where you once ran. "And when He got into the boat, he who had been demon-possessed begged

Him that he might be with Him. However, Jesus did not permit him, but said to him, 'Go home to your friends and tell them what great things the Lord has done for you, and how He has had compassion on you.' " (Mark 5:18-19 NKJV)

God is sending you back to make a rumor out of everyone's eternal prediction of you. When you resurface, the once true commentary then dissolves. It is obvious the 'new you' and the 'old you' cannot exist at the same time. When the time is right, be sure to resurface. People will need to see the grace of God.

ꕥꕥꕥ

Chapter 10

Repaired for Purpose

ꕥꕥꕥ

You were purposed so distinctly that you cannot be stopped!

DON'T THROW IT AWAY. REPAIR IT!

The purpose of an ax is to forcibly sever structures into two halves. Its purpose is not served until it is lifted, drawn, swung, and counted undefeated by any resistance. But should the handle on the ax head break, it would be foolish to throw the ax away. I understand logically you would think, "What else can I do with a disconnected piece of iron?" But all that is needed in the case of the severed ax head is a fitting reconstruction. Get it a handle! Always remember that purpose is decided by the creator and cannot be revised. Purpose is eternal. In other words, the wedge of iron is made for cutting and it cannot be used for anything else. It doesn't become a door stopper no matter how slender it is.

Please understand that every created thing is initiated with reason and a designed expectation in mind. Once established, purpose is so intentional until there aren't any alternatives. If purpose is ever challenged to a halt, restoration, not cancellation, is the only option. It would seem that after particular ruin, we'd be forsaken and fit for dilapidation. Sure, we can find other things to do with our lives in the name of "moving on" but purpose demands a restored "you" in order to succeed in your predestined calling.

REINSTATED

Here is what many have yet to acknowledge and accept, God will not issue a new purpose because you have gone off course. Not at all! Instead, He'll repair you to succeed in the thing to which He has called you to. You aren't here because of a simple heterosexual attraction where the right pick-up lines were dropped and sudden romance lighting made your parents irresistible to one another. You exist because the Almighty Creator deemed you necessary by reason. You are the word of the Lord: "So shall My word be that goes forth from my mouth; it shall not return to me void, but it shall accomplish what I please, and it shall prosper in the thing for which I sent it." (Isaiah 55:11 NKJV)

It is such a beautiful reality to know that God has planned sufficiently for our possible failures. Too many people result to discarding what they have paid top dollar for. But bloodshed is an expense too great to throw the ransomed away. Your price is absolutely unheard of: nails in His hands, nails in His feet, a crown of thorns upon His head, pierced in His side and stashed in a tomb to rise again. Anything paid with such expense is eternally redeemable.

In a "Three strikes. You're out!" kind of world, we aren't accustomed to expect anyone to exist after they have exhausted their opportunities to follow the rules and benefit from adhering to them. This is why grace is hard to grasp until we need it as our only hope. Grace is the spirit that understands how unrealistic the terms can be and creates a means or loophole for a pardon that is beyond fair. Grace considers the various circumstances surrounding the occasion of your fall, while "fair" is a stickler for the original agreement and found siding with the rules. Fair says you were warned and knew better. Fair has no feelings. Fair says you cannot be an exception unless everyone can be one, which would nullify the law altogether. For anything so brilliantly constructed to be nullified is humiliating, to say the least.

Most people would rather be fair until they have a need for grace. God knew this, which is why only he can forgive sin. If just anyone could forgive sin, no one would ever be forgiven. Forgiveness would become a lucrative industry, kind of like the papacy: a mere man in a box selling forgiveness who needs pardoning himself. If we had such power, we would be tempted to manipulate it.

My personal sentiment: thanks be unto God! I am so glad that Jesus created a clause for my freedom. It's always the clause that will shift the entire narrative and change the course of things. "For God did not send His Son into the world to condemn the world, but that the world through him might be saved." (John 3:17 NKJV) Through Him, I'm not only saved but when my salvation is stained and seemingly ruined, I am recovered and repaired for purpose. I pray you will testify of how grace brought you back. Otherwise, millions will give up where they should have reached up for help.

Here lies the end of my compilation of thoughts on the subject of recovery. Of all I have shared, the most important thing that you should know is that you don't recover yourself! Only a creator can service what they have purposed to function if it becomes dysfunctional or inactive.

Before you close this book, think about your story, your journey, your recovery. Remember in-depth what you felt and how you survived. You know the signs of a brewing scandal. You are well experienced for an entire population of people just like you. Go and rescue as many as you can!

CLOSING AFFIRMATIONS

The burden of secret sin is gone: Satan has nothing over my head. I am free through the power of the Son of God. | *John 8:36*

I am more than free: I am forgiven, my sins are drowned at sea. My reputation is restored through Jesus Christ. | *Rom 8:1*

I have rights to liberty: I will openly celebrate God's grace; telling the story from a redeemed point of view. | *Ps 103:1-5*

I am too loved of God to hide from anyone: All are welcome to see his sufficient grace on display. | *Gal 5:1*

By reading The Recovery Manual, I have overcome guilt and shame: I am both restored and reinstated. | *Col 1:14*

I have experienced the complete plot of the God and man relationship: My witness is credible: blessed, enticed, fallen, forgiven, redeemed, justified, glorified and presented faultless. | *John 3:16-17*

By the power of the Holy Spirit, I am transformed: I am not who or what I was. I resent old passions, preferences, lack of discipline and the habit of good behavior instead of full submission to the Holy Spirit. I now receive a new identity in Christ Jesus. | *2 Cor 5:17*

I will walk in the light: I lead others to the life I've found in Christ. | *1 John 1:7*

I am not ashamed of my experiences: Through them I have come to know God's boundless love. | *Rom 1:16*

I am a living, breathing recovery manual: My witness is someone else's deliverance. | *Ps 66:16*

www.ingramcontent.com/pod-product-compliance
Lightning Source LLC
LaVergne TN
LVHW050940080826
845145LV00004B/1342

* 9 7 8 0 5 7 8 2 4 7 5 9 5 *